KT-484-210

Contents

The meanings of the words
in **bold** can be found in the
COLOURFUL WORDS!
boxes throughout the book.

Introduction

The first 'clothes' were animal skins that hunters wrapped round themselves to keep warm. After a while people started to sew skins together with threads such as hairs from a horse's mane or tail. Colour was added by rubbing pigment into the animal skins. The earliest pigments came from plants and living creatures. A common colour was red ochre which came from the earth.

These scraps of wool, found during an archaeological dig, help us to learn what kinds of clothes have been worn in the past.

We wear clothes for many reasons. In cold countries people wear clothes to keep warm. In hot countries people choose garments which keep them cool. Sometimes we wear clothes to protect us or to show what our job is. We also wear clothes to look attractive and to let others know what sort of person we are. Sometimes people wear clothing which shows where they come from, or even whether they are married or not.

In the past there were sometimes laws which said that ordinary people could not wear certain types of dress. Rulers and wealthy people wore distinctive clothes and colours that

COLOUR IN
FASHION & COSTUME

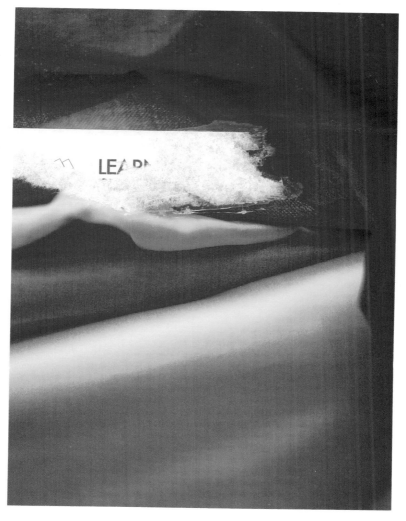

MORNA HINTON AND JOHN YORATH

Evans

Evans Brothers Limited

Published by Evans Brothers Limited
2A Portman Mansions
Chiltern Street
London W1M 1LE

First published 1995

Printed in Hong Kong by Dah Hua Printing Co. Ltd.

ISBN 0 237 51437 0

British Library Cataloguing in Publication Data.
A catalogue record for this book is available from the British
Library.

Acknowledgements

Editorial: Karen Ball
Managing Editor: Su Swallow
Design: TJ Graphics
Illustrations: Hardlines, Charlbury
Production: Jenny Mulvanny

The author and publishers would like to thank Rosemary
Harden, who acted as consultant on this book.

For permission to reproduce copyright material the author and publishers gratefully acknowledge the following:
Cover: (Main) Robert Harding Picture Library (inset) The Hutchinson Library
Title page: Pongees Limited
Contents page: Robert Harding Picture Library
page 6 — York Archaeological Trust; page 7 — (top) ZEFA, (bottom) Philip Craven, Robert Harding Picture Library; page 8 —
Musees Nationaux, Robert Harding Picture Library; page 9 — Mike Maidment, Life File, (bottom) London College of Fashion;
page 10 — Bruce Roberts, Science Photo Library; page 11 — The Image Bank; page 12 — Robert Harding Picture Library; page
13 — (top) The Bridgeman Art Library, (bottom) Robert Harding Picture Library; page 14 — (top) Bruce Coleman Limited,
(bottom) The Image Bank; page 15 — (top) Fritz Prenzel, Bruce Coleman Limited, (bottom) Robert Harding Picture Library; page
16 — David Austen, Bruce Coleman Limited; page 17 — (top) The Bridgeman Art Library, (bottom) Hulton Deutsch Collection;
page 18 — Mary Evans Picture Library; page 20 — (top) Graham Burns, Life File, (bottom) David M Campione, Science Photo
Library; page 21 — (top) Mary Evans Picture Library, (bottom) Michel Viard, Bruce Coleman Limited; page 22 — Sally Morgan,
Ecoscene; page 23 — (top) Hulton Deutsch Collection, (bottom) The Hamling Company, Bruce Oldfield page 24 — (top) Fraser
Hall, Bruce Coleman Limited, (bottom) Arthur D'Arazien, The Image Bank; page 25 — Sally Morgan, Ecoscene; page 26 — (top)
The Bridgeman Art Library, (bottom) James Carmichael Jr, NHPA; page 27 — Robert Harding Picture Library; page 28 — Robert
Harding Picture Library; page 29 — (top) Tony Morrison, South American Pictures, (bottom) Peter Newark's Western Americana;
page 30 — (top) Romilly Lockyer, The Image Bank, (bottom) Trip; page 31 — (top) Juliet Highet, Life File, (bottom) Trip; page
32 — (top) ZEFA, (bottom) Mary Evans Picture Library; page 33 — (top) Clive Barda, Performing Arts Library, (bottom) Mary
Evans Picture Library; page 34 — (top) Paul Van Riel, Robert Harding Picture Library, (bottom) The Bridgeman Art Library; page
35 — Sally Morgan, Ecoscene; page 36 — (top) Dr Charles Henneghien, Bruce Coleman Limited, (bottom) Victoria and Albert
Museum; page 38 — (top) The Bridgeman Art Library, (bottom) The Image Bank; page 39 — (top) Mary Evans Picture Library,
(bottom) Adam Woolfitt, Robert Harding Picture Library; page 40 — (top) Peter Newark's Western Americana, (bottom) Robert
Harding Picture Library; page 41 — Sally Morgan, Ecoscene; page 42 — Jane Burton, Bruce Coleman Limited; page 43 — (top)
Tim Fisher, Life File, (bottom) ZEFA; page 44 — (top) ZEFA, (bottom) Infocus International, The Image Bank; page 45 — Global
Hypercolor Inc.

Today, people wear clothes made from natural and man-made fabrics, in all kinds of colours.

were forbidden to ordinary people as a sign of their importance. In China from the 6th century to the beginning of the 20th century only the emperor was supposed to wear a certain shade of yellow.

In this book we are going to find out about how colour is used in all sorts of fashion and costume. We will be looking at clothes from around the world, both from the past and the present. We will discover how the materials used for fashion and costume are made, and how the colour is put into them.

The Masai people in Africa wear very bright colours and intricate jewellery.

The difference between fashion and costume

Fashion

Fashion did not always change as quickly as it does today. People think that fashions first started to change very frequently at the court of King Louis XIV. Louis XIV was King of France at the end of the 17th century. Life at court was one of leisure, and courtiers would amuse themselves by seeing who could wear the most fashionable clothes. Competition became so intense that courtiers were soon buying new outfits for each season of the year. Milliners (people who make hats) and dressmakers came to work near the court to satisfy the increasing demand for new garments. The idea of new fashions for each season began here, and today's fashion designers still bring out new collections of clothes for spring, summer, autumn and winter.

In the 19th century, technical developments and new machinery meant that patterns could be cut and sewn more quickly than ever before.

Fashion designers

Designers get ideas for new styles from many different places. They often look at garments from the past or clothes from other countries. They may get inspiration from a new type of fabric or a new

Louis XIV of France enjoyed wearing sumptuous clothes. His court at Versailles became a fashion arena in the 17th century.

dye. Fashion designers usually start by doing sketches of what they want the finished garment to look like. Then they work with a pattern cutter who turns their ideas into paper patterns. The pattern cutter starts off with standard pattern pieces for the different parts of a garment, for example the sleeves or the skirt. They make changes to these to fit in with the designer's ideas. They then make up a trial version of the garment in a cheap material like calico. This is called a toile. If necessary the pattern will be altered and then a final version is produced. Other designers prefer to start off by arranging a piece of fabric on a dummy. They cut and pin it until they have got the effect they want. This fabric may then be made up into a garment, or the designer may use it to make a paper pattern.

A fashion design student making sketches of his ideas for a new garment.

These fashion students are learning how to cut out paper patterns.

9

COLOURFUL WORDS!

fashion: a popular style of clothes

designer: some one who does drawings and plans which are used to make things

dye: a substance which colours things

costume: a style of dress associated with a particular region or time in history

People at work in a clothing factory, where garments are being mass produced. Machines cut the material in bulk before the pieces are stitched together.

Costume

Traditional **costume** is a style of clothes which has not changed very much over the years, and may be linked to a particular region or country. Although some people still wear traditional costume every day, it is usually only worn on special occasions and festivals.

National costume is an outfit which people wear when they want to show what country they come from. In the opening ceremony of the Olympic Games there is a parade where the athletes wear their country's colours. A folk costume is a traditional costume that is only worn in one area of a country. A country may have many folk costumes but just one national costume. It can be difficult to decide what the national costume should be. For example, the Jews who came back to live in Israel brought a great variety of folk costumes with them from the countries where they had been living before. The style that was eventually chosen for the national costume is based on folk costumes that were seen in Europe.

The clothes that actors and actresses wear when they perform in a film, play or television series are also called costumes. They have to be specially designed to work well as part of a production.

Actors in this stage production of an early 19th century novel wore costumes based on the style of clothes of that period in history.

Below: In 1988 the Olympic Games in Seoul, Korea were opened with people carrying the colours of the Olympic flag.

What are clothes made from?

Many different types of material are used to make clothes. Most contain fibres - fine, hair-like threads. Some fibres come from plants and animals. Some others are made from coal and oil. The fibres can be pressed together, woven or knitted to make a length of material.

Leather

People in cold climates need to cover themselves up to keep warm. Animal skins are an ideal material for protecting against the cold. As well as being warm, leather is also porous, which means that perspiration can escape. This makes it comfortable to wear.

In its natural state the skin of an animal does not make a good material as it would quickly rot. But if the skins are treated in a special way called tanning, they become supple and stretchy and will last much longer. The substance used for tanning is called **tannin**. Originally, natural tannin such as the bark of the oak tree was used, but today chemicals are also used.

First, the skin is soaked in chemicals to remove the hair. Once the fat and flesh are scraped off, the skin is ready for tanning. The substance used to tan the skin will decide the colour and properties of the finished leather. Tanning with chromium produces a greenish-blue leather which is very waterproof. Formaldehyde (obtained from wood) gives a white, washable leather.

The skin is soaked in a series of vats containing tanning liquids of increasing strengths. Some tanning processes can be completed in several hours. The more traditional methods can take many weeks. After tanning the leather is oiled to increase its suppleness. Suede leather is held against a moving wheel with a rough edge to give it its fluffy texture.

Leather being dyed in Morocco. The leather is soaked in a series of vats filled with dye to give it a vivid pink colour.

Linen

Linen is probably the oldest fabric we know of. In the Middle East, archaeologists have found spindle weights and equipment for spinning, together with fragments of linen fibres which date from 8000 to 6000 BC.

Linen is made from the fibres of the flax plant. The metre-long stems are pulled from the ground and then soaked to loosen the outside fibres from the woody core. Mechanical beaters then separate the fibres. They are combed, overlapped and drawn into a continuous ribbon of fibre. After that it can be woven. The most popular colour for linen is still its natural cream, as the high wax content in flax gives it a **sheen** that is attractive even without dyeing.

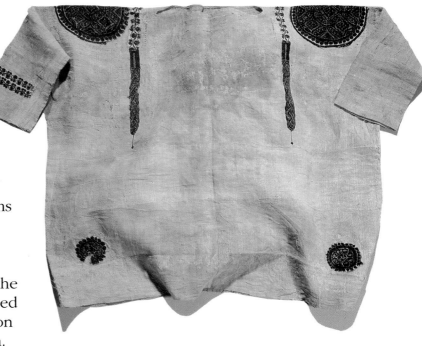

Linen is one of the earliest textiles made by people. This Egyptian tunic, made from linen and wool, is over 1400 years old.

These long stems of flax will be used to make linen.

13

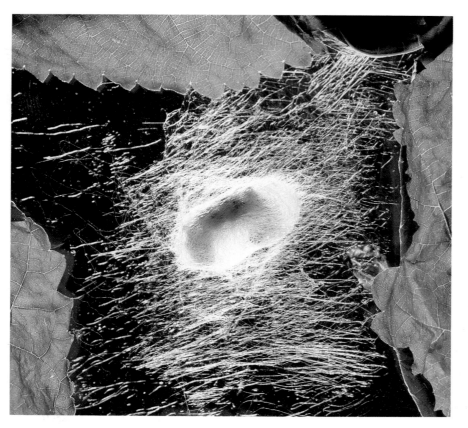

The fibres produced as this silkworm spins its cocoon will later be used to make silk fabric.

Silk is one of the finest natural fibres.

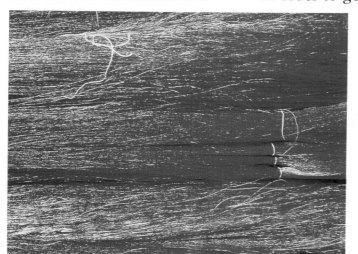

Silk

The Chinese discovered how to make silk over 4,500 years ago. They kept the method a secret until about the 5th century AD when it spread to India, Japan, Spain and Italy. No one really knows how the secret of silk manufacture was introduced into Europe. One story is that the Roman Emperor Justinian ordered two Persian monks to bring him the secret. They returned with some eggs of the silk moth hidden in a hollow bamboo stick.

The difficulty of manufacturing and the special properties of silk have always made it an expensive fabric. Most silk comes from the caterpillar of one type of moth (Bombyx mori) which only eats the leaves of the mulberry tree. When a caterpillar is ready to turn into a moth it wraps itself in a silky case called a cocoon. This protects it while it changes into a moth. It is the fibre which makes up the cocoon that is used to produce silk. A single cocoon can consist of a continuous silk fibre up to 1600 metres long. Even so, it takes over 100 cocoons to make a silk tie.

In order to get the silk from the cocoons they are placed in hot water to dissolve the sticky outer surface so that the fibre will unwind more easily. The cocoons are then lightly brushed to catch the ends of the fibres. Between five and seven fibres are then twisted together to make a single thread of raw silk which can be woven or knitted into a fabric.

Silk is a very light material. It is often made heavier to make it thicker and to help it hang better. Silk is very strong yet it is also elastic, which means that it keeps its shape well. Silk is a good insulator. Insulators do not let heat pass through them easily. This means that silk can keep

14

warm in cold weather because it stops body heat escaping. It also keeps you cool in warm weather because it stops heat from outside getting in.

Wool

Most wool comes from the hair of sheep. Other animals like goats, camels and llamas also have hair that can be spun and made into textiles.

When a sheep's fleece is first sheared the wool is dirty, greasy and lumpy. It is washed to remove the grease and dirt and then carded to remove the lumps and straighten the fibres so that they all point in the same direction. Sometimes wool is dyed at this stage and it is one of the few natural fibres that can be coloured before it has been turned into yarn.

Next it is spun (pulled and twisted) to become yarn. The yarn can be woven or knitted. A woven woollen fabric may have the surface fibres cut off to produce a smooth finish. Alternatively, you can brush the fibres up to produce a fluffy finish, as in a blanket.

Wool is hardwearing and light. It is also exceptionally warm, even when wet. It is used to make fire fighters' uniforms because it is slow to burn. When the fibres on the outside of woollen cloth come near a flame they burn and form a hard layer. This helps to stop the fibres beneath from catching alight.

Wool fibres are covered with tiny overlapping scales. When they are pressed together very tightly they lock to produce a dense and almost water-proof textile known as felt. Unlike woven woollen fabric, felt does not fray when cut. It can be moulded and is often used for hats.

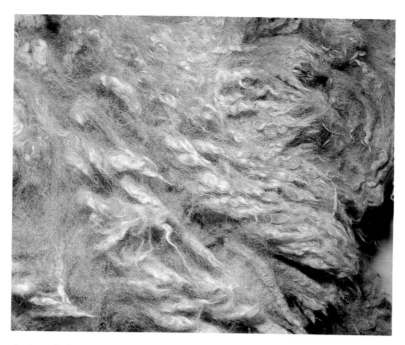

A sheep's fleece needs to be cleaned thoroughly before it can be made into wool.

Wool does not catch fire easily and is an essential part of a fire fighter's protective clothing.

15

Cotton

The first country to grow cotton on a large scale was India. Between 1500 BC and the 15th century AD it was the world's most important producer of high quality cotton cloth. From the 7th century AD European countries started to produce cotton too.

Cotton comes from a plant which needs a warm climate and moderate rainfall. This means that it will only grow in certain parts of the world. After the cotton plant has flowered a seed pod (or boll) forms. When ripe, this opens to reveal the fluffy white cotton fibres (known as lint) to which the seeds are attached. When cotton thread is made, the first thing that is done is ginning. Ginning removes the seeds, which are used in cattle feed and cooking oils. The lint is then carded in the same way as wool to line up the fibres and remove the very short ones. After that it is spun into a yarn. Finally, two or more yarns may be twisted together to make a much stronger thread or are combined with yarns of other fibres such as wool or silk. Untreated cotton is usually a creamy off-white colour, but because it is highly absorbent a wide range of colours can be applied to it.

These cotton harvesters in Australia use modern farming machinery to pick the cotton on their land.

Synthetic fibres

People have always admired the unique qualities of silk. In 1664 the British scientist, Robert Hooke had the idea of making cheaper, artificial silk. However, it was over 200 years before any progress was made. Then, in 1884, another British scientist, Joseph Swan, was working on the problem of producing a filament for his electric light bulb. He was experimenting with a liquid called nitrocellulose solution which contained plant extracts and nitric acid. He developed a method of squeezing it through tiny holes to form thin threads called filaments. He then treated the fibres with chemicals to get rid of the acid. He had made a synthetic fibre but did not appreciate how useful it would be for textiles.

It was at the Paris Exhibition in 1889 that artificial silk was seen for the first time.

Five years later the first example of artificial silk was shown at the Paris Exhibition. It was called Chadonnet silk, because it was invented by Count Hilaire de Chadonnet. The process was very similar to that used by Joseph Swan. Chadonnet's method was simple and involved little waste but it was slow and expensive. Chadonnet silk was later called rayon. By 1892, another method of producing an artificial fibre was developed by a British firm. It was called viscose and by the beginning of the 20th century it was in common use, as it still is today. The essential ingredient of both rayon and viscose is wood pulp. A mixture of chemicals is added to the pulp to make a sticky liquid. This is filtered and then squeezed through fine nozzles. It comes out as a dry fibre which is wound on to reels. It is then spun into a yarn.

Up until the 1930s stockings were often made from silk. With the invention of nylon, stockings could be made that were hardwearing and affordable, causing a revolution in women's clothing.

Nylon was invented in America in 1930. Nylon is made from liquid chemicals spun through tiny jets and allowed to dry in a stream of cool air. These fibres are gathered together to form a single strand which is then stretched. It was first produced commercially in 1939 and shortly after was used to make women's stockings. They had the texture of silk but were much more hardwearing. Nylon is also much stronger than rayon and is less likely to rot or be attacked by insects.

There is now a whole range of synthetic fibres. Polyester is one of the strongest and most crease-resistant, while Lycra

COLOURFUL WORDS!

tannin: substance made from dried and powdered leaves for treating and colouring leather

sheen: a reflective quality in material

During the Industrial Revolution mechanical looms were introduced into factories. Working conditions were harsh and often dangerous.

is an elastic material used in many types of clothing, including underwear and socks. Synthetic fibres can be mixed with plant and animal fibres to produce new materials. Some synthetic fibres are used for protective clothing. Kevlon is used to make bullet-proof vests for the police. It is so strong that it is impossible to cut with scissors. Glass fibre is used to make spacesuits for astronauts. It is fire-proof and extremely strong.

Weaving

Threads can be woven together to produce cloth on a loom. Vertical rows of threads (the warp) are held taut on the loom. The weaver winds another thread (the weft) in and out of the warp threads using a shuttle. Different coloured threads can be used to produce attractive patterns.

Looms can be very simple and portable or large and complicated machines. The earliest looms were operated by hand. Mechanical looms were invented in the late 18th century. They could weave cloth much more quickly and cheaply than hand weavers. Thousands of weavers were put out of work by these machines.

COLOURFUL THINGS TO DO!

Make a simple loom

You will need a strong piece of card about 20cm by 15cm, a blunt-ended needle with a large eye, and some wool, string or raffia. As well as using different colours, you can make interesting effects by using threads with different textures such as raffia or string. You can even weave with twigs or dried grasses.

1 Cut a series of V-shaped notches about 1cm apart at both ends of the card.

2 Fix one end of a long length of wool to the back of the card with sticky tape. Beginning at the top left hand notch, wind the thread down the front of the card, around the bottom left hand notch and back up the front into the next notch. Wind the wool tightly but not so tightly that the card bends.

3 Continue doing this, working your way across the card until you have wound the wool around every notch. Secure the remaining end to the back of the card with another piece of sticky tape. These are your warp threads.

4 Thread the blunt-ended needle. Starting from one side pass the needle alternately over and under the warp threads until you have reached the other side of the card.

5 When you reach the last warp thread of a row pass the needle around that thread and continue in the other direction. Pull the thread so that it is not loose.

6 Each time you finish a row use a comb with widely spaced teeth to pack the thread against the other rows.

How is colour put into clothes?

There are many ways of adding colour to clothes. Fabric can be woven using different coloured threads. Designs can be embroidered or printed on to the fabric. The most common way of adding colour to clothes is by dyeing them. Fibres can be dyed at any stage in their manufacture. Synthetic fibres are usually coloured before they are spun. Natural fibres can be dyed before or after they are spun. Sometimes textiles are dyed after they have been woven.

Natural dyes

The fruits, stems, leaves and roots of many plants contain natural dyes. If fabric is soaked in a liquid containing juices from these plants it becomes a different colour. The colours obtained with this simple method are rarely **fast** – the colour quickly fades in bright light or when the cloth is washed.

There have been many attempts to make natural dyes stay in the cloth longer by using substances such as salt, vinegar, blood, saliva, egg white, lemon juice and even water in which rusty nails had been soaked. Any substance which helps fabric absorb and hold the dye is called a mordant. Different mordants used with the same dye can produce a variety of shades and even completely different colours. If dye made from carrot tops is used with an alum mordant it will produce a yellow colour. If copper sulphate is used as the mordant it gives a green. Bilberry fruits dye wool pink, but if the wool is

Top: This wool has been coloured before spinning, so that different colours can be combined in one thread.

Above: In this textile factory, colouring is done after the material has been woven.

first soaked in salty water it will turn a blue-grey colour. Most
mordants originally came from plant material such as rushes,
moss and fruit peels. Nowadays, chemicals are used. Nearly
all natural dyes need a mordant to produce a fast colour.
There are some however, like tea and walnut shells, which
can make strong, permanent dyes without a mordant.

Up to about 100 years ago all dyes were obtained from
plants and animals. Some colours were easier to get than
others. Browns and yellows were the easiest. It was hard to
make a bright green even though it is the commonest colour
in nature. The two oldest plant dyes are indigo and woad.
Indigo was made by fermenting the indigo plant in a bath of
fruit and stale urine. The pale yellow liquid was then used to
dye wool and cotton. When the fabric was dried it turned
blue. Woad is a plant belonging to the cabbage family which
produces a blue dye. Another very old dye is madder. The
madder plant is used to make a crimson coloured dye. When
explorers first visited the Americas in the 15th century they
brought back plants and trees unknown elsewhere in the
world. Some of these produced new natural dyes.
Logwood, the bark of a Brazilian tree, produced a
deep blue-black which is still used.

Some natural dyes come from animals. The
Romans used part of a type of whelk (a shellfish),
to make Tyrian purple. Scarlet was obtained from
cochineal - the dried bodies of a tiny insect
(Coccus cacti) which lives on cacti in places like
Mexico. Until 1954 the British Guards' uniforms were
dyed scarlet using cochineal.

Some fruits and nuts can be used to
make natural dyes
(below: a walnut).

COLOURFUL THINGS TO DO!

Investigating natural dyes

SAFETY WARNING: Some plants and fruits are poisonous. Use only those which you know are safe. If you are not sure assume they are poisonous. Most natural dyestuffs need to be boiled in water to release their colour. An adult should help you with this.

You will need rubber gloves, an apron, an old saucepan (which will not be used for cooking food), a clean wooden stick, a selection of small squares of different types of white fabric (try to find at least one natural and one synthetic fabric).
   Most natural dyes will not be fast but that does not matter. You are experimenting to find out what colours are produced from various plant materials and how different textiles take the colour.

Some natural dyes you might like to experiment with:

tea	mustard	onion skins
coffee	turmeric	red cabbage
leaves	soot	bark

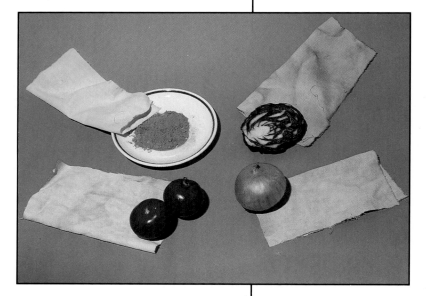

1 Half fill the saucepan with cold water and add the dyestuff.
2 Bring to the boil and simmer over a low heat. Tea will release its colour immediately the water boils. Others, like the onion skins, will take longer.
3 Turn off the heat. Place small squares of different textiles in the liquid. Stir with the wooden stick.
4 Rinse the squares of material in cold water and allow to dry.
5 Make a note of the colour of each square once it is dry. Which natural dye is the most effective? Which textile absorbs dye best?

Synthetic dyes

Colours changed in the late 1850s when Henry Perkins, a young British scientist, accidentally discovered a new dye while working in his laboratory at home. He noticed that the liquid he was working with turned everything purple and the stains would not come out. 'Perkins mauve' was the first of a huge range of synthetic dyes which would eventually replace almost all natural dyes. Other dyes followed and the range of colours increased. Nowadays almost any colour can be obtained chemically. Dyes made from chemicals are less likely to wash out or fade in bright sunlight. The raw materials for synthetic dyes first came from coal tar. Coal tar is produced when coal is heated in a closed, airless container. Chemicals are separated from the coal tar and these are then used to make the synthetic dyes.

But the increased use of chemical dyes has not been good news for everyone. When substitutes were found for indigo and madder there was no longer a need to grow the plants. As a result, thousands of farmers in India lost their livelihood.

Henry Perkins was the first person to discover synthetic dyes.

The invention of synthetic dyes has allowed the fashion industry to use a whole range of bright colours.

These women are transferring a design on to material, using a method called Batik, which uses wax and dye.

Printing

Colour is often applied to the surface of fabric by a printing process. The simplest of these is block printing. A wooden or metal block, on which a design has been carved, is inked and then pressed on to the cloth. Traditional Indian prints are still made in this way but it is a slow and highly skilled process. Nowadays most textiles are printed using machines that have raised designs on huge rollers. The rollers can apply as many as sixteen colours to the cloth at high speed. Screen printing, where ink is pressed through a stencil, is also widely used. After printing the ink on the cloth it has to be fixed (usually by heating) to make the colour fast.

In modern textile factories, large rollers are machine-cut to print textiles. This man is putting the finishing touches to a textile printing roll.

Bleaching

Sometimes a white fabric is needed. In the past textiles were spread out in fields to **bleach** in the sunlight. In 1774 chlorine (a gas which could be dissolved in water) was discovered. Chlorine bleached textiles much more quickly. Today textiles can be coated with **fluorescent** substances to make them appear white. This method is particularly used on synthetic fibres that would be grey if left untreated. Modern detergents contain fluorescent specks to replace those washed off the fibres and keep the fabric looking white.

COLOURFUL THINGS TO DO!

Material art

Intricate patterns can be made when dyeing material and it is not difficult to create your own original designs using a stencil. You will need wallpaper paste, powder paint, a plastic bowl, an apron and rubber gloves, a sponge, card, scissors and a piece of white cotton.

1 Pencil in your design on the card. If you have a large piece of material to print it may be best to repeat a single motif (for example, stars or moon shapes) so that the stencil may be used over and over again until all the material is printed.

2 Once you have finished drawing the design, cut it out of the card. The simpler the design, the easier it will be to cut out.

3 Mix your dye by adding powder paint to the wallpaper paste until you have the colour you want. Use a plastic bowl and wear an apron and rubber gloves.

4 Place the stencil over the material and apply the dye with the sponge. Do not apply too much dye or it will seep into the material and blur the edges of the shapes.

5 When you remove the stencil you will see the printed material. Repeat the process as many times as is needed to cover all the material.

6 Finally, hang the material over a radiator or somewhere warm to dry.

Colour in traditional costume

Wall paintings such as this from the tomb of the King of Thebes show us how Egyptians dressed.

Murex shellfish were used by the Romans to make purple dye.

Ancient Egypt

The ancient Egyptians usually wore draped styles of clothing. Draped clothes are made of lengths of material wrapped around the body and held in place with belts and ties. Ancient Egyptian costume did not change very much for about 3,000 years. Before 1500 BC, most people just wore a loin cloth known as a schenti. This was a piece of cloth wrapped round the waist and between the legs. It was kept in place with a wide belt. Later a long, fringed tunic was worn over the schenti. Women sometimes wore a short cloak as well. The ancient Egyptians used linen, made from the flax which grew in Egypt, to make clothes as it was light and cool. It was also naturally white, which was a sacred colour in Egyptian religion.

The Romans

The Romans wore draped clothes too. Some men wore a toga, with a loin cloth or tunic underneath. Togas were made from a very large semi-circle of cloth. It was not a very practical style of clothing to work in so only rich people wore togas. Colour was used to show a person's rank. Magistrates and politicians wore white. Generals in the army wore purple and gold. The emperor wore purple. Purple came from a very expensive dye made from part of a shellfish, and only people who were considered important were allowed to wear purple.

Roman women wore a long tunic. Women could wear almost any colour: red, yellow and blue were the most popular. Their clothes were made of silk and cotton and were sometimes decorated with embroidery and fringes. Over the tunic women wore a second, long-sleeved tunic called a stola. For going out they wore a cloak. The cloak was a bit like a toga but it was made of a rectangle of cloth rather than a semi-circle.

Saris in India

In India people still wear many styles of traditional costume as well as Western-style clothes. Traditional Indian costume is comfortable to wear in hot weather. The colours for Indian costume can vary depending on what time of year it is. At harvest time people wear yellow and red, the colours of the sun, and green, the colour of plants. The festival of Diwali which is in October or November is the festival of light. People like to wear lots of bright, rich colours for Diwali.

The red colour in this bride's sari is traditionally worn at Indian weddings as a symbol of fertility.

Indian women have worn saris for nearly 2,000 years. The sari is a long piece of material which is worn draped round the body. It is draped in various ways depending on where the woman comes from. Patterns, colours and fabrics are different in different areas too.

When women get married they wear a very elaborate sari. It is usually red and is worn over a green choli (a short-sleeved bodice). The red sari is a present from the bride's family. Red is the colour of fertility in India. Wearing a red sari means that the bride hopes to have children.

Indian men often wear a type of wrapped skirt called a lungi to relax in at home. For going out they may wear a long fitted jacket with a high collar called a choga, with narrow trousers. The choga is normally made of white linen. For very special occasions it may be made of richly-coloured brocade.

Palestinian embroidery

Palestinians live in the country we call Israel. It used to be called Palestine. Many Palestinians have been forced to leave the towns and villages where they were born. They now live in refugee camps. Their traditional costume is an important way of remembering their home and some of them wear it all the time. The traditional dresses of Palestinian women are either white or dark blue. Other colours are also used to let people know where the

Palestinian women use intricate embroidery to decorate their traditional costume.

woman's home village was. The dresses are decorated with embroidery and panels of material which are sewn on. The more panels a woman has on her dress the richer she is. The bits of material are in **contrasting** colours such as red, green and yellow. This means that people can easily see how many panels there are and therefore how rich the woman is.

Many Palestinian men wear a black and white head cloth called a keffiyeh. It is held in place with a band called an aqual. It was originally worn by a group of Palestinians called the Bedouin. The Bedouin are nomads who live in the desert. The keffiyeh became popular for all Palestinian men after their leader, Yassar Arafat, started wearing it. Nowadays people all over the world wear it, but not always as a head cloth. It makes a good scarf.

Costume in Africa

Many African people still dress in traditional styles. Women often wear a piece of fabric wrapped and draped around their body. It is a bit like an Indian sari. Like the sari it is suitable for hot countries. In Kenya this piece of fabric is called a kanga. In West Africa it is called a wrapper and is made of colourful patterned cloth. Women wear the wrappers with lots of gold jewellery and bead necklaces. They also wear matching pieces of fabric tied round their heads. In Nigeria these are called gele.

Loose robes are an important part of traditional costume for African men. In northern Nigeria it is traditional for Hausa men to wear flowing, ankle-length robes. They are beautifully embroidered with colourful patterns. Underneath the robes the men wear baggy trousers gathered at the ankles.

Traditional costume does not always stay exactly the same. Since the late 1970s people in Africa have worn clothes which are traditional in style but made of new woven fabrics with lurex in them. Lurex is a shiny plastic thread which looks like metal. Fabrics which have lurex in them are sometimes called 'mirror in the sun'. We now think of them as traditional fabrics because they have been used constantly for about 20 years.

Men in Nigeria often wear long flowing robes in bright colours.

Guatemalan red

Some of the most colourful traditional costume in South America can be found in Guatemala. The majority of people there still wear traditional dress. Red is a very popular colour, especially for the head ties that the women wear and the belts worn by men. This is because Guatemala used to produce large quantities of the natural red dye cochineal. Although synthetic dyes have now replaced natural dyes, red has stayed popular. Women in Guatemala wear long, narrow, ankle-length skirts. The skirts are either made from patterned material or they are embroidered. The embroidery is often green or purple. The colours of the skirts are different for different regions. The Mam women who live in the west of Guatemala wear yellow silk skirts with stripes.

Men wear multi-coloured striped shirts with trousers, belts and short jackets. The jackets are made of black or white wool and are decorated with embroidery. The trousers may be embroidered or made of stripy fabric.

Red is an important colour in Guatamelan costume. Originally, the dye would have been made from a tiny insect called cochineal.

Brightly coloured blankets

The Navajo people are one of many tribes of native Americans who lived in America before the arrival of Europeans in the 17th century. An important item in their traditional costume is a blanket. Both men and women wear blankets that they wrap round their shoulders like shawls. The earliest patterns on the blankets were stripes of colour. The traditional colours were white, brown, dark blue and red, which come from natural plant dyes. In the late 19th century the Navajo started to make very brightly coloured blankets, using new chemical dyes to make bright colours. The blankets had zig-zag stripes and small triangles on them in contrasting colours.

A painting of Navajo Indians, showing their traditional blankets and a weaver at work.

Tartan designs vary widely and can identify which clan the wearer belongs to.

Because of their bright colours and patterns the blankets became known as 'eye-dazzlers'. Nowadays the Navajo sometimes wear blankets for ceremonial occasions although they do not wear them every day.

Highland kilts

In Scotland the national costume is made of a **checked** woollen material called tartan. It was originally worn as a single length of material wrapped around the waist and held in place with a belt. The end of the material was draped over the shoulder and the upper body. At night people used the material as a blanket. By the middle of the 18th century the skirt had become a separate garment. This is what we know today as the kilt. It is worn by men. Women wear a length of tartan called a plaid over their shoulder as part of their national costume. The colour and pattern of the tartan let you know what clan (family group) somebody is from.

Germany

In Germany the colours used in folk costumes sometimes tell you whether some one is married or not. In the Black Forest region women wear flat straw hats decorated with pom poms as part of their folk costume. Unmarried girls have red pom poms, married women have black ones. In the south of Germany men wear embroidered braces. If the embroidery is white it means they are married. If it is red then they are single. People in Germany wear their folk costume for dancing and festivals.

Kimonos are an important part of Japanese national costume.

Japanese kimonos

The kimono is the best-known part of the Japanese national costume. It is a kind of long coat which is worn by both men and women with a sash. A very wide sash called an obi goes round the waist and is carefully tied in an elaborate bow at the back. The obi and the kimono are usually of contrasting patterns and colours. Several kimono may be worn in layers. In the past this was a way of showing how rich you were. Sometimes people wore so many that they could hardly move! The lining of silk kimonos is usually red. The red shows at the hem, which is rolled up and padded. The padding makes the kimono hang better. Nowadays kimonos may be worn for weddings and other special occasions. People may also wear a short kimono for relaxing in at home.

Fashion and traditional costume

In West Africa today it is fashionable to wear traditional styles of clothing. A popular garment is a loose robe called a boubou. Boubous are nearly always made out of vivid cotton and are decorated with eye-catching embroidery. In Ivory Coast women wear dresses made of modern, printed cloth with traditional designs. The designs frequently show well-known stories and proverbs.

Some Africans and West Indians living in Europe and America like to wear clothes which remind them of their African roots. Multi-coloured kente cloth is popular. Kente cloth was first made in the Ashanti region of Ghana. It is made from narrow strips of hand-woven fabric which are sewn together to make one large piece. It is patterned with stripes of different thicknesses in colours like bright blue, light green, golden yellow and dark red. People may wear a large piece of kente cloth draped round them in a traditional style or buy Western-style clothes which use it as a trimming.

In India, Pakistan and Bangladesh designers often choose colours which are traditional in their region. For example, in the northwestern state of Rajasthan designers use a lot of bright pink and purple. This is because Rajasthan used to be ruled by princes. Pink and purple are colours associated with royalty in India.

COLOURFUL WORDS!

contrasting: describes colours that are very different, such as black and white

checked: having a pattern of small squares

Kente cloth is a traditional African textile that can now be found in Western fashions.

The pinks and purples that some of these women wear are traditionally associated with royalty in Rajastan.

31

Colour in theatre costume

Colour is used to create mood and atmosphere in theatre productions. In addition, the colours of a character's costume and make-up give you clues about what sort of person they are. Many costume designers start by choosing colours with well-known associations. For example, an evil character may wear dark clothes while a good character is more likely to be dressed in white. But in Western theatre there are no hard and fast rules about what colours go with different types of character.

In traditional Chinese theatre there are special colours for particular characters. If an actor has his face coloured purple it means he is a calm, loyal official. On the other hand, if his face is white then he is a sly and cunning character.

In Chinese theatre colours often have special meanings.

Famous costumes

There are some drama costumes that we all recognize straight away. They might be centuries old, or they may be from the latest popular film. Colour is often important in helping us to recognize and remember certain characters and what they wear.

In the 16th century an Italian theatre called 'Commedia dell'Arte' toured the country performing in the streets. The costumes of many of today's street entertainers come from these first outdoor performers. One of their most famous characters, the Harlequin, is still popular today. He can be seen in a very brightly **patterned** outfit made up of many diamond shapes in different colours. In fact, this colourful costume had very humble beginnings. As street entertainers, the 'Commedia dell'Arte' could not afford expensive costumes, and the Harlequin's outfit was originally made from many different scraps of material sewn together.

The Harlequin's costume was first invented in the 16th century and is still worn today.

Other entertainers wear very simple colours. Mime artists traditionally wear only black and white. Originally this was because they didn't want colourful costumes to take attention away from their mime. Today, black and white has become a 'uniform' that almost all mime artists wear.

In more recent times, costumes from a popular film can become familiar all over the world. In the Superman films, the character Superman wears a bright red and blue costume. These exciting colours are used in his outfit to express the energy and 'superhuman' powers of the character. If he had been dressed in greys and browns, people might not have been so willing to believe that he could save the world!

Challenging colours

In the 19th century costume designers were expected to make theatre costumes historically accurate in order to make the play as truthful as possible. In recent years, however, theatres have used costume to challenge our ideas about a play.

Shakespearian actors have been put in costumes that vary from nuclear age uniforms to nightclub outfits – all in order to make us look at these old plays in a new light.

Interestingly, though, an updated version of a play or opera does not necessarily make it more colourful. Many historical costumes are far more ornate and decorative than the clothes we wear today. Some people prefer to see plays and operas in historical costume because it is more colourful.

Sometimes colour helps us to understand who a character is. A recent production of *The Wind in the Willows*, adapted by Alan Bennett, had actors and actresses playing animals. Instead of putting them in animal costumes, their outfits were designed very carefully using colour to suggest different animals. 'Toady' was dressed in a shocking green wig and glasses and a white and green blazer. The colour green helped the audience to recognize what animal the actor was supposed to be.

The influence of theatre costume on fashion

Theatre costumes sometimes influence fashion. In 1909 a Russian ballet company called the Ballets Russes came to Paris. The Parisian audiences fell in love with their style of dancing and, most of all, with their colourful costumes and sets. Many of the most **vibrant** designs were by a painter called Leon Bakst. Bakst loved to use rich, glowing colours like mustard, violet, **jade**, yellow and **crimson**. He always included lots of different shades in each costume. The French fashion designer Paul Poiret had been using similar colour combinations for several years. When the Ballets Russes arrived people wanted to buy Poiret's designs because they were like Leon Bakst's costumes. Lots of other fashion designers began to copy Poiret's style.

patterned: something decorated with an arrangement of shapes and colours

vibrant: brightly coloured

crimson: a deep red colour

jade: a bright blue-green

▲ How else could this actor be made to look like a toad?

A design by Bakst for the Ballets Russes dancer Nijinsky. The Russian company's colourful costumes inspired designers to experiment with bold new colours.

Colour in fashion

Shocking pink, created by designer Elsa Schiaparelli, is still a very popular colour.

Rossetti's *Reverie*. Paintings such as this depicted an alternative fashion in the 19th century for softer colours in clothes.

Popular colours are not always decided by the fashion industry. Some of the colours that we take for granted in our clothes today have an interesting history. Science, politics and religion have all played their part in the colour of clothes in the past and what we still wear today.

New colours are introduced into fashion all the time as new dyes are created. If a fashion designer likes a new colour, he or she can make it popular all over the world. In the 1930s the Italian fashion designer Elsa Schiaparelli introduced a vivid new colour which she named 'shocking pink'. In 1951 another designer, the Frenchman Jacques Fath, invented another new pink. He called it 'hot pink'. He designed silk clothes in 'hot pink' and sold lots of them. In 1952 he came up with an even brighter pink which he called 'very hot pink'. These different **shades** of pink became very fashionable and were used for sheets, towels, curtains and lipstick as well as for clothes.

It was in the middle of the 19th century that the first chemical dyes were produced. Before then all dyes had come from plants or minerals. Purple had always been hard to make with natural dyes. Chemical purple dyes were some of the first to be invented. Soon there were many new shades of purple dye available. One of the most popular was a reddish purple called magenta. Chemical dyes were also invented for other colours. It became fashionable for European women in the second half of the 19th century to wear these vivid new colours. In the early 1870s dresses where the **bodice** was a different colour to the skirt were very popular. Patterned and plain materials were often used together on one dress so that even more colour could be added. Not everyone liked these bold new colours, especially in Britain. British artists like Dante Gabriel Rossetti and designers like William Morris started a fashion for softer, more natural colours. People who thought they were artistic often dressed in these sorts of colours.

COLOURFUL THINGS TO DO!

A scientific way of mixing colour

Anyone can mix colours to invent a new one – the problem is remembering how you did it! If you mix your paints scientifically you should be able to make exactly the same colour again. To do this you will need two small amounts of liquid paint of two different colours (red and yellow work well for this), two medicine droppers (you can buy these cheaply from a chemist), two saucers, a fine paintbrush, some paper, and a pencil.

1 Fill each medicine dropper with one colour of paint.

2 Divide your paper into two columns. Write 'red' at the top of one column and 'yellow' at the top of the other.

3 Squeeze six drops of yellow paint on to the saucer. Write a '6' in the column marked 'yellow'.

4 Squeeze one drop of red paint on to the saucer and mix the two colours together with the paintbrush. Write a '1' in the column marked 'red'.

5 Add drops of colour, remembering to record on your paper how many drops of each colour you used.

6 When you have mixed a colour you like, add up the columns on your paper. The totals will tell you how many drops of each colour were needed to make the shade you mixed.

7 Keep the saucer with your favourite colour but wash the brush.

8 On the clean saucer squeeze the correct number of drops to repeat your favourite colour. Use the brush to mix the paints together.

Did your second colour match your first one? How could you make this a more accurate method of mixing colours?

Greek statues such as these influenced the style of clothes in France after the Revolution.

Politics and fashion

Political events sometimes influence what colours are fashionable. At the end of the 18th century the people of France became caught up in what is now known as 'The French Revolution'. The working class of France had been left starving by their King and Queen. Angry mobs in Paris executed many members of the ruling class to set up a new kind of government. It was hoped that the new democratic government would give ordinary people a say in how their country was run.

The earliest known democracy was in Ancient Greece. The French people who supported the revolution took this first democratic society as their model and began to dress in a similar way. Their ideas about Greek costume came from stone statues which had survived since Ancient Greek times. Many of these statues were made of white marble and showed people wearing simple, close-fitting clothes. The French began to wear a lot of white in imitation of what they knew about Greek costume, and also as a reaction against the **sumptuous** clothes the nobility had worn before them. Soon nearly every woman in France and the rest of Europe was wearing slim, white dresses. They were made of thin, cotton fabrics like muslin but these were not suitable for the cool climate of northern Europe and women had to wear wool shawls with them to keep warm. The interesting thing is that people in Ancient Greece did not all wear white as the French thought. Poor people often did because they were not allowed to dye their clothes but rich people wore coloured and patterned clothes. The stone statues had originally been painted in bright colours. Over the years the paint chipped off until there was none left. So the fashion for white after the French Revolution was based on a mistake!

This 19th-century drawing of French dress illustrates the fashion for loose narrow skirts.

COLOURFUL THINGS TO DO!

Colour combinations

Fashion designers spend a lot of time selecting combinations of colours which they think people will like. There are even companies which specialise in forecasting what colour combinations people will be wearing next year. They produce brochures which are used by fashion companies. You can choose your own colour combinations with this colour matcher. You will need a pair of scissors, some stiff white card, coloured pencils, felt pens or paints, and a ruler and pencil.

1 Cut three strips of white card about 24cm long and 2cm wide.

2 Mark out 12 boxes 2cm deep on each strip. Leave the ends blank.

3 Use felt pens, crayons or paints to colour each box a different colour or shade. You could choose your colours at random or make one strip contain only shades of red, one of blue and one of yellow.

4 On a piece of white card about 24cm by 7cm ask an adult to make three pairs of slits 2cm apart with a sharp knife.

5 Thread one of your colour strips through each pair of slits.

6 By sliding the strips you can change the colours which show in the three windows.

7 Experiment with different colour combinations to find those which you like most and those you like least.

This portrait of a noble lady shows how large and impractical ruffs became at the height of their fashion.

Though their trainers are modern, these Amish children are still expected to wear traditional clothes in plain colours.

Fashions against bright colours

Spain was one of the most important European powers in the 16th century and became the leader of fashion. Spanish garments were severe-looking and almost always in black and other dark shades. In the mid-16th century men and women started to wear white ruffs. These were bands of linen which were pleated, or folded like a concertina. Ruffs became so huge that they often had to be supported by wearing a piece of card or wire behind your head.

Very strict Christians called Puritans continued to wear dark-coloured clothes even after brighter shades came back into fashion. Puritans believed it was vain to wear colourful garments. Even today some strict Christians wear very sombre colours. The Amish are a group of Christians who live in North America. They try to live as simply as possible and dress in styles of clothes from the 19th century in restrained colours.

At the end of the 18th century a man called Beau

Brummell became a great leader of fashion in Britain. He was a friend of the Prince of Wales, and dressed very smartly, preferring plain fabrics. He nearly always wore a dark blue coat and a spotless white tie called a cravat. Men all over Europe admired Beau Brummel for his immaculate presentation and were soon following his style. During the 19th century men continued to prefer plain, simple clothes for most occasions. The colours became very dark. This **trend** continued into the 20th century. It became the accepted way of dressing for men in the West and was the beginning of the suit as we know it today.

Since the 1950s men in the West have begun to wear a greater variety of colours again, although many men still wear dark suits for work. Often the only colourful thing a man wears at work is his tie. In the mid-1960s there was a fashion for very wide ties known as kipper ties. These were often of a flamboyant design in bold, bright colours.

Beau Brummel was a leader of 18th century fashion.

Dark colours have become a uniform for most male office workers.

39

The story of blue jeans

Since the 1950s blue jeans have become fashionable all over the world. When they were first made in the middle of the 19th century they were work clothes. Jeans were invented by a German man called Levi Strauss who lived in America. In 1850 he went to the town of Eldorado near San Francisco on the west coast of America where people were digging for gold. He took lots of **canvas** with him. He thought he would be able to sell it to the gold-diggers for tents and covers for their wagons. But when he got there he found that what they really needed was tough, hard-wearing trousers. So Levi Strauss got a tailor to make some out of this brown tent canvas. He sold them to the gold-diggers and was soon able to start a shop in San Francisco. After a while he started to make his trousers out of a fabric which was even stronger than canvas. It was called 'serge de Nîmes' after the town of Nîmes in France where it was made. In America the fabric began to be called denim which comes from the words 'de Nîmes'. Levi Strauss dyed the denim blue using indigo dye. He added copper rivets to make the trousers even stronger. They were called jeans because the denim was brought to

Jeans were first made from tent canvas for gold-diggers in the Californian gold rush.

Today jeans are one of the most popular items of clothing around the world.

America on boats where the sailors were mainly Genoese. They came from the Italian city of Genoa. Jeans is a shortened form of Genoese. The original jeans would gradually fade from dark to light blue as they were worn and washed. Nowadays jeans can be bought ready-faded and in a whole range of colours.

COLOURFUL WORDS!

shade: a darker or lighter version of a colour

bodice: top part of a dress

sumptuous: splendid or expensive

trend: a fashion for something

canvas: a heavy cloth made from cotton

tailor: somebody who makes clothes

COLOURFUL THINGS TO DO!

A colour scrapbook

Fashion designers collect all sorts of things to give them ideas for their designs. They may pin them to a noticeboard or stick them in a scrapbook. Why don't you make your own colour scrapbook? You will need ten sheets of paper, a hole punch, a ruler, scissors, string, and some glue.

I Punch four evenly-spaced holes on the long left-hand side of the pieces of paper. Thick cartridge paper is best. Make sure the holes are always in the same place. Tie the sheets of paper together by passing the string through the holes and knotting it.

2 You now have your scrapbook. Inside there is room for you to have one page each for red, blue, yellow, green, orange, purple, black and white. Cut out clothes that you like from magazines and stick them on the appropriate page. You could add scraps of fabric as well. You may sometimes find it quite difficult to decide what page something should go on!

Useful colours in clothes

The flower mantis disguises itself with a green and yellow pattern that blends in with the plant it lives on.

Camouflage colours

Animals are sometimes coloured so they blend into their surroundings. This helps keep them safe from predators. Human beings use the same idea for **camouflage** clothing. Camouflage clothes make people hard to see. The first camouflage colour was khaki. It has been widely used for European soldiers' uniforms since the First World War. In the late 19th century the British army out in India had their uniforms made of local khaki-coloured cotton. In the Indian language Urdu, khaki means dust-coloured. Khaki uniforms blended in well with the scenery in a hot, dusty country like India. Although khaki was originally beige it came to mean a whole range of colours from beige to brown to green. Back in Europe khaki-coloured material was used for car coats at the beginning of the 20th century. People needed protective clothing for motoring because the first cars were open-topped. Khaki coats were practical because they did not show the dirt. Nowadays camouflage uniforms for soldiers use special disruptive patterns. These patterns break up the surface and make it hard to see the outline of a shape. Different colours are used depending on where the uniforms will be worn. Yellows and browns would be used for desert uniforms, while white is used for Arctic military suits.

This soldier's uniform uses camouflage to keep him hidden in the jungle.

Some restaurant uniforms use strong bright colours to create a lively atmosphere.

Colour and identity

Colour in clothing can help to give a group of people a sense of identity. Sports teams all over the world can be identified because they wear their team colours. In Nigeria family members frequently wear clothes made of the same material for occasions like weddings. The identical patterns and colours reinforce the feeling of being a family. Groups of Nigerian women who belong to the same social club or religious group often use the same fabric for their clothes too. They may even get a fabric designed especially for them.

Some employers like their staff to wear a uniform. This helps the public know who to ask if they need help. Sometimes work uniforms match the colours of the workplace. This is often seen in shops and restaurants. An atmosphere can be created which fits in with the company's image. Fast food restaurants often use very bright primary colours for their staff's uniforms. The restaurants are decorated in the same colours. Bright colours like this are supposed to make people want to eat quickly. This is good for the restaurant because it means that they can serve more customers.

Chadors are worn by women in Saudi Arabia to help them stay cool in the heat.

This motorcyclist's jacket reflects light in the dark, so he can be seen on the roads.

Colour and climate

Many people in hot countries wear a lot of white and light colours. However, not everyone who lives in a hot climate wears white. The Tuareg people of the Sahara desert wear a long piece of cotton called a tanguelmoust wrapped round their head and body. It is often white but it can also be a bright colour like green or blue. Arab women in places like Saudi Arabia wear an ankle-length black robe called a chador. Although black **absorbs** heat and light it also **deflects** glare from the sun.

Coded clothes

In Western countries people have traditionally worn loose, light-coloured clothes to keep cool in the summer. However, in Australia a new system of labelling clothes has been set up recommending darker colours. For the first time you can buy clothes with number coded labels that tell you what are the safest colours to wear in the sun. The best clothes for hot weather are those made from tightly woven fabrics and dark colours. These are said to give the best protection from ultraviolet radiation, which is a major cause of skin cancer.

Colour and safety

Colour in clothes can help keep us safe. Miners all over the world wear denim overalls in light, bright colours. This makes them easy to see in the dim light of the mine. Traffic policemen and -women wear reflective clothing so that motorists can see them easily. If you cycle at night it is a good idea to wear a reflective band or bib.

COLOURFUL THINGS TO DO!

Design a uniform

As we have seen, uniforms can influence the moods of people both wearing and seeing the clothes. You might try designing a uniform for staff at a place where customers are encouraged to have a good time. This could be a theme park or funfair. What colours would you choose to make people feel happy? Look through your own wardrobe or old magazines to see which colours seem most exciting in clothes.

As well as designing for colour you will have to bear in mind the comfort of the wearer and the practical demands that will be made on the clothes.

camouflage: the ability to blend into surroundings for disguise or concealment

absorbs: to take in or soak up light or liquid

deflects: to bounce back from a surface

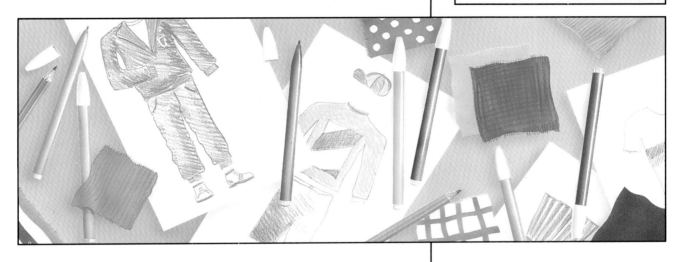

Glow in the dark fashion!

Although fluorescent materials were originally developed with safety in mind, they have also been adopted by the fashion industry to make exciting new clothes. The T-shirt seen here is dyed using special crystals that absorb light and then slowly emit it back out in the dark. The glow from clothing such as this can last for up to ten hours.

Is there any way you can think of to make safety gear more interesting to wear? How could you use fluorescent material in other clothes?

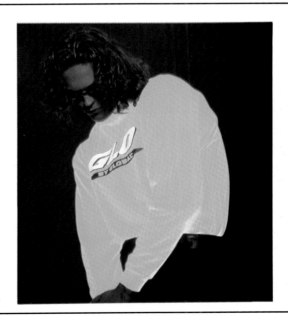

The latest in fashion technology — a glow in the dark sweater.

45

Index

Books to read

Colour in Communication, Wonderful World of Colour, Sally and Adrian Morgan, (Evans Brothers)

Clothes through the Ages: a history of costume, vol.1, Discoverers Series, Jean-Louis Besson, (Moonlight Publishing)

Costumes and Clothes, Jean Cooke, (Wayland)

Fabric Art, Fresh Starts Series, John Lancaster, (Franklin Watts)

The Timeline of World Costume from Fig Leaf to Street Fashion, Claudia Muller, (Thames and Hudson)

Theatrical Costumes, Costumes and Clothes Series, Miriam Moss, (Wayland)

Traditional Costumes, Costumes and Clothes Series, Miriam Moss, (Wayland)